Rem Koolhaas: conversations with students

Rem Koolhaas

CONVERSATIONS WITH STUDENTS

ARCHITECTURE AT RICE 30

SECOND EDITION

RICE UNIVERSITY SCHOOL OF ARCHITECTURE, HOUSTON, TEXAS

PRINCETON ARCHITECTURAL PRESS, NEW YORK

1996

Edited by Sanford Kwinter
Designed by Sze Tsung Leong

Published by Rice School of Architecture; Lars Lerup, Dean
and Princeton Architectural Press; Kevin C. Lippert, publisher

Photography: George O. Jackson, pp. 38, 62; Sze Tsung Leong,
pp. 12-13, 16-18, 41, 43, 57; Hisao Suzuki, pp. 23, 26-30;
Hans Werlemann, pp. 19, 20, 31-35.
Executive editor: Dung Ngo
Special thanks: Rem Koolhaas and OMA, Ann C. Urban, Mark
Lamster, Rebeca Méndez.
Printed and bound in the United States

©1996 Rice University School of Architecture
Architecture at Rice Publications
6100 South Main, Houston, Texas 77251-1892
713 527 4864

and

Princeton Architectural Press
37 East Seventh Street, New York, NY 10003
212 995 9620

ISBN: 1-885232-02-0
Library of Congress Cataloguing in Publication Data is available
from the publisher

contents

Earlier and more clearly than any contemporary architect, Rem Koolhaas, like Manfredo Tafuri before him, recognized that architecture has been eclipsed by the Metropolis. While other architects have settled for being mere decorators of the scaffold of commerce, Koolhaas remains among the last holdouts to seek *new* possibilities and locuses for architecture. Though this struggle might at first seem quixotic, a form of obsessive delirium, it now appears, with the imminent arrival of his opus magnum *S,M,L,XL*, that Koolhaas may have found a temporary respite for architecture within the very concept of the extra-large, that is, in Bigness, or in the Metropolitan itself.

The decision to re-edit this issue of *Architecture at Rice* reflects our belief that in its terse compactness it prefigures bigger things to come. It also serves as an inspiration for the revitalization of the *Architecture at*

Rice series. Koolhaas's spontaneous and incisive comments about Houston (the "Lite City") reconfirmed my own sense that, for us at Rice, Houston could offer a marvelous laboratory for our own experiments and attempts to forge ahead.

The revitalization of this publication symbolizes in many ways that the Rice School of Architecture fully feels the challenge of the Metropolis, and like Koolhaas, knows well that the struggle is not lost. This exhilarating work directs at architecture a much needed defiance, and as such, it serves as our mascot.

Lars Lerup

Dean

Rice School of Architecture

Lecture 1/21/91

Architecture is a dangerous profession for several reasons. It is especially dangerous if you have a name like Office for Metropolitan Architecture—a very pretentious name, compared to which almost any realization may be found wanting. There is, for instance, a house in Paris that we are now building, one whose swimming pool happens to be on axis with the Eiffel Tower, yet this simple fact does not make the building metropolitan, even if the French seem to think so.

Architecture is a dangerous profession also because it is incredibly difficult and debilitating. In this Paris house there is a simple idea: that it might be nice to have an apartment that floats in the air. Our whole office of 35 people was intellectually engaged for over two years to make this simple idea a reality. In those two years there was no possibility for us to also think.

Finally, architecture is a dangerous profession because it is a poisonous mixture of impotence and omnipotence, in the sense that the architect almost invariably harbors megalo-

maniacal dreams that depend upon others, and upon circumstances, to impose and to realize those fantasies and
dreams. I will talk tonight about some moments in our office's
career when, through those random circumstances and
accidents, the pretension of our name came close to being
realized, in the sense that in a series of programs we
were offered the opportunity to investigate what, today, a
metropolitan architecture might be.

In this sequence, the program for the Parc de La Villette
was a very important moment, because it allowed us to investigate the theme of congestion, for us the key ingredient
of any metropolitan architecture or project. For the first time
after our preoccupation with New York, we tried to imagine
what congestion at the end of the 20th century in Europe could
mean. The concept of this park was drawn from the American
skyscraper, where a series of activities are superimposed
in one single building. For the Parc de La Villette we took this
model and spread it horizontally over the surface to make a

park that was a catalog of 40 or 50 different activities
arranged like floors, horizontally over the entire surface of the
park. In this way we could realize the congestion or density
of the skyscraper without referring or resorting to building or
to architecture in any way. Two years earlier, the same site
had been the subject of another competition, for which
Leon Krier had proposed a famous project that was all walls,
streets, plazas, et cetera. It set the tone for a whole movement for the restoration of the European city, reimposing and
reinventing it as a nostalgic model.

What I want to discuss now is a series of more recent
projects that reflect a new condition in Europe itself—a condition that has something to do with 1992, with a new energy,
a new way of thinking, and a new confidence in Europe. This
inevitably goes hand in hand with an enormous explosion
of scale, previously unthinkable in Europe. What is interesting
is that this scale is now to be planted, or fitted, into a European context where history is an important issue.

The first of these projects is a city hall for The Hague:
a proposal to inject a building program of two million square
feet in the medieval center of The Hague. In other words, it
was an impossible program, a fact that we both realized, and
suggested in our design.

What was fascinating about this series of projects, which
dates from the summer of 1989, was that certain themes
developed in *Delirious New York* and the analyses we had made
there of American architecture suddenly turned out to have
relevance in a European context. Four of these themes inform
or determine the issues these projects deal with. All are
connected to an escalation or quantum leap in scale and to the
achievement of a certain critical mass—when a building,
through its size alone, enters a completely different realm
of architecture.

The first observation is that, in a building beyond a certain
size, the scale becomes so enormous and the distance
between center and perimeter, or core and skin, becomes so

vast that the exterior can no longer hope to make any precise disclosure about the interior. In other words, the
humanist relationship between exterior and interior, based
upon an expectation that the exterior will make certain disclosures and revelations about the interior, is broken.
The two become completely autonomous, separate projects,
to be pursued independently, with no apparent connection.

The second characteristic of this new, mutant scale
of architecture is the fact that within such a building, the
distances between one component and another, between
one programmatic entity and another, also become
so enormous that there is an autonomy or independence of
spatial elements.

The third, and still largely unexplored, phenomenon is
the performance of the elevator. The role the elevator plays in
a building of such enormous scale and its revolutionary
potential make it a very dangerous instrument for architects.
It completely undermines, annihilates, and ridicules an

enormous part of our architectural abilities. It ridicules our compositional instincts, annihilates our education, and undermines the doctrine that there must always be an architectural means to shape transitions. The great achievement of the elevator is its ability to mechanically establish connections within a building without any recourse to architecture. Where architecture, in order to make connections, has to go through incredibly complicated gestures, the elevator simply ridicules, bypassing all our knowledge, and establishes connection mechanically.

The fourth, most confusing index of this enormous scale is that the building is impressive simply through its mass, through its appearance, and through the dumb fact of its own existence. It appears impressive, if not beautiful, whether the architect influences it or not. The amoral position of such a building, the effect of the scale alone and its intimidating volume, is something that is very disturbing to architects, who always think that only they can make the uniform substance of a building beautiful. The fact that a big building is itself an impressive element accounts for the impressiveness of certain spectacles, such as La Défense or the skyline of Houston, where the total effect is unbelievably impressive even though it is hard to identify impressive individual architectures.

Based on these four observations, in the summer of 1989 we worked on some projects whose programs themselves made us aware of certain connections, of certain almost revolutionary conditions, that were beginning to take place in Europe as a whole.

Zeebrugge Sea Terminal, Belgium, 1989

The first building was a ferry terminal on the North Sea.
Because of the future Channel Tunnel the owners of the ferry
lines between England and the Continent were becoming
alarmed, and were therefore improving their facilities through
the creation of incredibly palatial terminals. Crossing the
Channel on ship is meant to appear vastly more attractive than
the rather sinister experience of travelling by train in the
tunnel. One of those companies asked for a colossal building,
on the order of two million square feet, on the Belgian
coast in the town of Zeebrugge. The building was to accom-
modate a very complex program of traffic and simultaneous
access to four boats, as well as an enormous amount of
restaurant, casino, hotel, and convention space. We found
the greatest difficulty in this location was to imagine,
in this landscape, and on a pier built two miles into the sea
surrounded with sheds and cranes, an architecture that
could separate itself from the surroundings yet also symbol-
ize, or represent, the specific needs of the client.

For the first time in our careers as architects, we found ourselves confronted with very artistic choices in that the only judgment we could make was no longer functionally based, because the problem was too complex to be analyzed in a rational manner. It was a myth that had to be assembled. Halfway into the competition we found ourselves judging whether one shape was more beautiful than another. Our criticism of one shape was that it was too much like a human head, and we settled, four days before the end of the competition, on a shape formed by the intersection of a cone and a sphere.

The lower third of the building is organized in a continuous spiral that first contains access facilities, then traffic facilities, and then, continuing up the ramp, an enormous parking element. But then suddenly the building becomes more interesting because the utilitarian parts stop abruptly and the spiral shape turns into a restaurant. At first it is a rough restaurant for truckers, but as it continues up, it becomes

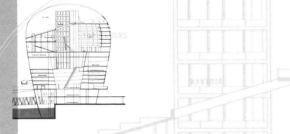

more sophisticated and luxurious. Also, this is the first
moment, in a building which is otherwise very closed, that the
public is allowed to enjoy the view and be confronted with
both the expanse of the water and the possibility of looking
back at the Belgian coast. The ramp goes on, and a black
office building cleaves the building in two. An enormous void
separates two autonomous and independent volumes, one
a hotel and the other a convention center, on the side closer to
the sea. At the top is an enormous amphitheater from which
you can see all the way to England on a beautiful day.

What was fascinating in this investigation of the implications of the very big building in Europe was the shift in
priorities, and the discovery that issues that in smaller buildings play minor roles take on, at this new scale, an absolutely
crucial importance. One of those issues was structure.
Working with the engineers Ove Arup and Partners in London,
we proposed two different options to the client, each of
which had structural and even philosophical implications.

One option was to prefabricate the building and erect it quickly. By erecting a fireproof steel skeleton, we could cover the shape with chicken wire and spray on concrete. We would then be able to assemble the building in record time—approximately 42 months—but the price would be a certain flimsiness to the building, and therefore a certain unreality. There was, however, another option in which the construction time could remain one of the attractions of the building. We proposed that a crew of just 24 Belgians begin the building in reinforced concrete and simply grow old with the construction. The minimal progress that the building would make, in the interval of different rides on the ships, would be a strong part of the building's appeal, while after 40 or 50 years, the Belgian construction workers, by then old men, would finally reach the top. The price of this option was that construction was very slow, but the end product would be a completely authentic and real building.

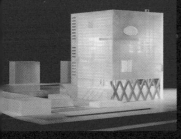

Bibliothèque de France, Paris, 1989

The second building we did that summer was a competition in which the issue of the very big building was literally a theme of the competition, a library in Paris. It was to be Mitterand's last project, not a single library but a combination of five completely separate libraries. One was a cinemathèque that was to contain every film and video made since 1940, so in the program there was an equivalence between word and image as a theme. The second was a library of recent acquisitions, the third a reference library, the fourth a catalogue library containing all the catalogues of the world, and the fifth a scientific library. So the problem of the building was not only the scale—some three million square feet—but also the fact that the program was composed of five completely different libraries, each with its own idiosyncrasies and its own public. The library was to be built on the Seine, in an isolated area near Bercy, surrounded by housing towers from the 1960s and 1970s. The site, an old railroad yard, was literally colossal, 750 feet deep and 1500 feet long, and there were no planning

proposals for the library's insertion in the urban context other
than the French predilection for an axis, to be placed somewhere in the middle and continue across the Seine on a
pedestrian bridge. The building also had to be low, on average
240 feet, with certain exceptions allowed when it was important for the impact or symbolism of the building.

What we found was two different conditions: one was that
of the public rooms, and the other was that of storage,
which took 60 percent of the program. At first we thought we
could put all the storage in one thin socle, which would
form a podium. The five different libraries could then be char-
acterized by different forms, buildings, or interventions
on this podium. Soon we became bored and irritated by the
discourse of an architecture in which you always have to
design yourself out of an essentially architectural problem. We
became irritated at thinking that we had to imagine five
different libraries as five forms, one funny, one ugly, one beautiful, and so on. In other words, we became more and more

resistant to the norms of an architecture in which everything has to be resolved through the invention of form.
We sought for the first time to really invent, architecturally.

Eventually, a sketch we made for another building acquired interest and relevance. The diagram suggested that, for an architectural program with two components, one very boring and the other very special, maybe it was possible to organize the boring part of the program as a series of regular and repetitive floors. Then you could create or invent special conditions, not as a positive thing, in terms of form, but simply by leaving out the boring part of the building. Maybe it was possible to articulate the most important part of the building simply as absence of building, as a kind of refusal to build. These spaces could then be seen as excavations in what otherwise appears as a solid mass. In this instance, all the storage could be seen as one enormous cube, and then all the public spaces could simply be excavated.

You could then develop a certain logic of the parts—the

most public could be in the lowest part of the building, the
part that needed the most darkness could be at the core—
and in an intriguing way, programmatic suggestions began to
emerge. It became clear, looking at the section, that if you
conceive the major elements of the building as voids, you are
allowed much greater potential. The floor could come
around, turn up, become a wall, then a ceiling, turn around on
itself, become another wall and then the floor again. In
other words, you could have a void space that makes a loop-
the-loop as part of the spectrum of interiors.

At regular intervals there would be a vertical core, and then
all you had to do was make sure that every void space was
intersected at least once by one of the elevators. At that point
it became easy to design the building, because we knew
from the beginning that the plan was square, that there would
always be nine elevators, that each void must be intersected with an elevator, and that differing needs for light would
dictate the different character of the public rooms.

The difficulty was to imagine a structure that could support the mass of the storage, as well as the voids, in their weightlessness. A structure based upon points would ruin the voids. At the same time, the massive building program, combined with the height restrictions, presented a problem because the thickness of the floors, which can take up as much as 60 percent of the section, would give the building an excessive height. In a European context, this makes the building indigestible. So we introduced, in a very brutal way, parallel walls, sometimes two meters or more thick, in which we could run all the services. The distance between the walls was 40 feet, so it was sufficient simply to puncture the wall to service the adjoining air space. The advantage to this was that the structure could support the mass required for storage, as well as the voids, which could be simply cutout of the walls. Because the wall in its entirety would act as a colossal deep beam, 240 feet deep, the cut-outs could be taken almost with impunity from any point in the building.

Since the whole building acted as a beam, it was possible to imagine that somewhere at the lower level there could be one open floor, entirely empty, where the public could be received.

We achieved something quite important in the lower part of the building, because in most highrise buildings the lower parts are full of the enormous inheritance of everything that comes from above. In this building, the construction system allowed the bottom to have the same freedom found at the top. What was striking was the similarity between the plans and the sections. Our source of greatest pleasure was the fact that we could make these voids and discover with relative freshness the correct and exciting form for each library, and have them co-exist without interfering with one another.

In the lower level there are auditoria, like pebbles in an empty space. We wanted to have one huge hall at this level where masses could meet. The library will have on the order of four times the current number of visitors at

Beaubourg. In other words, real masses and a real metropolitan scale. To orient these masses, the elevator shafts—
isolated poles in this vast open plaza—could be electric signs
whose words, texts, or songs represent the destinations
of the individual elevators. All these letters, moving up, would
make the building seem to hover, entirely supported by
the alphabet.

When we came up with this hypothesis, we invited our
intellectual friends—architects, colleagues, and writers—to
show them our latest thinking. Our ideas were received
with an absolutely stony silence, which furthered our resolve
to take the idea and go further. The library of recent
acquisitions would be one horizontal space. The library for
videos would be an enormous sloping space that would be a
continuous amphitheater. The third, a reference library
and reading room, was a continuous spiral making three
revolutions and connecting five floors. The library of cata-
logs was egg-shaped, and it intersected with the façade.

The suggestion was made that this building contained all the libraries in the world. It would have an enormous window on the city of Paris, which itself is also a library, the ultimate library. Finally, at the top is a space so complicated that it turns inside out, doing a loop-the-loop. This room is so long that it has windows at the end and at the top. Since this is the scientific library, we thought we could have the most experimental spaces there.

Once we had thought of the building this way, there was one big unresolved issue: the exterior. We had to find a series of elevations for this bizarre assembly. We thought we could use glass in such a way that it sometimes made disclosures. Sometimes, like a cloud, it would obscure what was happening behind, and at other times it would simply block what happened by being opaque. We thought the elevations could almost have the effect of nature, in the sense of its formlessness and its changing aspect.

ZKM Center for Art and Media Technology,
Karlsruhe, Germany, 1989

The last project is a museum for media in Karlsruhe, Germany.
The museum is to serve as a laboratory, a university, and
a theatre of media. Our first thought of Karlsruhe was of an
idyllic baroque city, but like all cities it is now filled with
highways, railways, and autobahns. The site is exactly at the
interface of the old city and the new city. I made a diagram
in which I saw that it was important to introduce a series of
axes, knowing that the only way anyone could really enjoy
the baroque city was from above. As a result, three axes inform
the project: an axis of connection to the city; one of circulation within the building; and finally, a vertical axis, which
delivers the pleasure of seeing the baroque city.

The exciting thing about the buildings is that structure
plays a very important role. We imagined a system of enormous trusses that could span from wall to wall. These trusses
would be so deep that they could include the whole floor.
Therefore it was possible for one floor to be completely determined by structure and for the next to remain completely free.

It became possible to change and manipulate the trusses for artistic effect, to bring about a kind of emotion or empathy, in terms of the structure of the building. In section, one can see how the increasing theatricality of the museum is consummated, to the point that what you have is a single stack of events. The first is the theater, followed by two floors of laboratories, one floor of a lecture hall, and then two museum floors.

All of this would happen at the center of the building, in one central tower, which would be surrounded by four different zones: one for public circulation; one for offices; one for technology that, like a stage tower, extends the full height of the building; and one that is a series of balconies. These four zones would simply wrap around the central core of the building.

On the lowest floor is the theater, above which are two floors of laboratories. The theater is a space where the whole spectrum between classical theater and completely simulated theater will be presented, so it is a space where every single plane can be seen as a surface for projection; in that

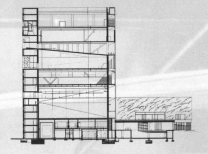

sense the entire space can be completely manipulated. There could be real decors, as well as electronic decors, and decors that occur as projections. Above this are the laboratory floors, which are sometimes completely determined by structure and at other times completely free. As in the case of the library, this would create enormous freedom for planning the building and allow for an enormous variety of spaces.

Continuing through the museum, the next floor is completely isolated from the outside, so there is no reference to the outside world. The following floor is sloped in its entirety, so there is a natural tendency toward an amphitheatre. When there is a need for privacy, there is a yellow silk curtain, but even then there is a sense of floating, with the view of the city, even during the lecture. The top floors have a classical organization, so the building starts with a very experimental organization below and becomes almost Schinkelesque at the top. Here, at the roof, you can see Karlsruhe by day or night and enjoy the baroque city.

Another interesting thing about the museum for media is
that what is inside can be seen almost as an evasion of public
life. At the same time the word, represented on the exterior
of the building, presents to the outside a certain kind of message, in the most vulgar communicative sense. This is also
something that we accommodated in the museum.

On the exterior, one elevation has a thin, transparent
metallic surface that can serve as a projection screen and can
completely transform the building's character. Some of the
activities taking place in the laboratories can be directly projected on the outside. On the north side there is a system
of public circulation that can be projected on the façade, with
people climbing to different levels of the museum. At the
top would be the auditorium, a kind of floating island by night.
The next side would be the office zone, and finally the
technical zone.

What is interesting about media is that it presents itself
as an enormous meal that looks incredibly satisfying but in

fact always leaves you hungry. The implied curse, of course,
is that we want it to tell us something we don't already know.
There is an incredible pressure for the media to always
change, in terms of both its content and its form. What is difficult about doing a museum for media is that curse of
continuously accelerating events, combined with the problems
of creating real space as well as space that is virtual,
ephemeral, or destructible.

Seminar 1/21/91

What is your reaction to Houston today? I was especially
surprised by the complete radicalization of the downtown area; I have
never seen any American city where the downtown is so intensely built up
with new construction. As a counterpart to this new building there is a
complete evacuation, a complete erasure of any building more than ten or
fifteen years old. This in itself is amazing, and I have to suspend any
kind of judgment. This landscape of isolated towers is really more pure,
and in a way more ideological, than anything I have ever seen. One
thing that I find astonishing in American cities is that, in an interval of ten
years, a city completely changes its concept, its visual aspect. It literally
changes overnight, and this happens every ten years, and I find that completely astonishing.

We need a new glue to hold a city like Houston together.
Where do we go from here? I am doing
a book called *The Contemporary City* that compares one European example,
the new cities around Paris; one American example, Atlanta; and one Asian
example, Tokyo or maybe Seoul. It's a book that I did more as research for
myself than out of any eagerness to make a statement. Its main inspiration
is the baffling discovery that Americans are talking about the problems of
their cities, Europeans are talking about the problems of their cities, Asians
are talking about the problems of their cities, but if you look at these cities,
there is almost no difference between them. There is an area here in
Houston called Post Oak. This same phenomenon, separate objects strand-
ed fairly randomly without any glue in a more or less objective landscape,
is now true of large parts of Europe, America, and Asia. Since these conditions exist in these different contexts, with different political systems,
different economies, and different ideologies, it isn't those external and
obvious factors that makes them similar.

I wanted to do a book to document this similarity and suggest to the
Europeans that there is no reason for complacency and to the Americans
that there was no reason for despair. As I was writing, the emphasis
changed from documenting these phenomena to trying to interpret what
they mean to architecture. If all these cities are now so similar, it probably
means that people want them that way. It also means that there is an
enormous difference, a bifurcation almost, between the ambitions of the
architect and the actual ambitions of society. I think the least these things

represent is an enormous freedom: freedom from formal coherence, freedom from having to simulate a community, freedom from behavioral patterns.

Maybe we should stop looking for any kind of glue to hold cities together. In cities like Houston, people have found, largely without the help of architects, other forms of coherence. In Atlanta, for instance, there is a very common model, which is to simply sling a wall around an area, put up a gate, and hire guards. Of course it's not an architectural coherence and it's not the kind of coherence that we as architects are indoctrinated to respect, but it is a very strong kind of coherence.

Do these cities work better
in Europe
because of their pedestrian life?

In the new towns around Paris,
you don't see anyone walking.
When we talk about Paris, we are still obsessed with the central city,
where, indeed people walk, but, if you look in numerical terms, there are
now more Parisians living in the new towns than there are living in
the center of Paris. In the new towns, the distances are similar to those in
Houston, and I think that the only reason to walk there would probably be
poverty, more than any eagerness to walk. When you talk about glue
that holds it together, there is in Marne-la-Vallée a complex that begins
with a large building by Ricardo Bofill—one of his best, an incredible
heap. The complex, an incredible monument of social housing now mostly
occupied by Vietnamese, is entered through a supermarket and then a
series of other ambitious housing complexes. There is an enormous
emphasis on pedestrian axes, malls, pedestrian vistas, and arcades. The
more emphasis there is on the pedestrian, the more vacant such an
area becomes, and the more pathetic the ambition of the architect when
compared to the obvious refusal of people to inhabit these spaces the way
the architect wants them to.

I am sure this splintering is a dangerous thing. But it is a thing that
architects can do nothing about. The whole thrust of the profession, its
education, its ethos, is still firmly rooted in a very nostalgic analysis. A profession that is in essence only whining will never be able to make a
constructive contribution. It is curious to me that even the firms that most

successfully and most guiltlessly contribute to those kind of explosions still talk about pedestrian areas, connections, et cetera—things that their buildings absolutely fail to produce or deliver. We are dangerously crippled in a rhetoric and a language that falls painfully short, and we cannot even begin to analyze what is really going on.

The role of the architect in this phenomenon is almost negligible. The only thing that architects do, from time to time, is to create within those given circumstances more or less masterful buildings. There is an unbelievable overestimation of the power of architecture in terms of the good it can do, but even more, in terms of the bad it has done or can do. Architects have been instrumental in this assessment through their accusation of modern architecture. In the vicious complaints and criticisms they developed in the 1960s and 1970s, and in howling with the wolves against the imagined misdeeds of modernism, I think architects have, in a very important way, weakened their own profession.

***Would you say
that it is economic forces and developers
that are
leading us to this new order?*** We are confronted
with enormous projects,
often without interesting
programs, or stimulating architectural substance. Our society continuously reinvents its needs, and these needs are real. Simply to blame the
developer for this kind of architecture is partly justified, but it's also a
refusal to come to terms with it. Maybe it is simply an inability to imagine
what kind of architecture could digest those indigestible lumps.

You say that these problems can't be solved by architects, but at some level we have to wonder where they can be solved. I am not saying they can't be solved by architects. Architects can be very important too, but I think architects are unable to read the mutations that take place and to reinterpret certain phenomena as being new versions, incarnations, or manifestations of phenomena they previously knew in architectural terms. I think we are still stuck with this idea of the street and the plaza as a public domain, but the public domain is radically changing. I don't want to respond in clichés, but with television and the media and a whole series of other inventions, you could say that the public domain is lost. But you could also say it's now so pervasive it does not need physical articulation any more. I think the truth is somewhere in between. But we as architects still look at it in terms of a nostalgic model, and in an incredibly moralistic sense, refuse signs of its being reinvented in other more populist or more commercial terms.

I hate to talk as a kind of thinker or philosopher, but this is my sense, purely as a reflection of the kind of work we are asked to do. It is not a philosophical comment, but simply the result of some issues being registered with such frequency that we have to begin to take them seriously. In that sense, we can shed an enormous amount of responsibility, but we can also find an incredible number of problems to work with. You can go to these cities and bemoan the absence of a public realm, but as architects it is better for us to bemoan the utter incompetence of the buildings, the absurdity of their implementation, and the cynicism of their production by some specific architect. It is not to be imagined that in such a context you are helpless. For example, in Atlanta there are examples of these Rockefeller Centers in the jungle that actually have great conviction and power.

***Are there current planning efforts that respond
to these new manifestations?*** I wonder

whether there is a planning discipline that can take the form of inter-
pretation and intelligent enabling. Perhaps that is a more relevant or plausi-
ble role for planning in the near future. Houston is now at a point where
planning will for the first time start to play a formal role in the life of
the city. I think it is very important not to invent or impose this discredited
apparatus, this nostalgic notion of the public realm, on these old and
recognizable models of mass architecture, and instead try to see it in a
more recent light.

One thing that I see is the enormous danger in beginning to plan or in
introducing planning. It could easily go against the vitality of a city
like Houston, so I think what has to be done is a very precise analysis of
what is happening and, if possible, why. Then a retroactive concept
could be extrapolated, or form the basis of a forward-looking extrapolation.
I really worry, for instance, that one of the first gestures might be to
limit any future destruction, and to fill the voids and make it look like a
recognizable city.

That is, in a way, a weakness in being an architect at the moment.
There is simply an incredibly impoverished catalog of models, and
at the same time there is the infinite imposition of these few models on
almost any situation.

In Europe it seems to be governments that drive architectural production, and in America it is developers. Actually the reality lies somewhere between. Planning is not just the attempt to do something immediately, but an attempt to imagine or create conditions that allow different forms of density, or different scenarios to develop. Once you start to investigate that, you can be completely daunted by the task.

One of the things that is most counterproductive in Europe, and even in America, for executing the task of planning is the terrifying phenomenon of the change in political systems every four years. In that sense the whole tone can change overnight: if the Socialists lose a few seats and the Greens gain a few, not a single tree can be felled. In that sense, then, in America the developers are a bit too powerful, and in Europe, politics are too powerful. Paradoxically, these two forms of power have surprisingly similar results. The kind of jagged line of development can be related in America to the power of certain developers, and in Europe to the relative power of the different political parties.

Our project in Lille operates under constraints similar to yours, because it is finally a commercial project and has a developer. It is not as if Europe is a carte blanche situation. I don't see why this same more or less enlightened interest can't exist in America, especially since in America, a montage of different economic and public elements to make a project viable has been a tradition rather than the exception. Look at Rockefeller Center, for instance. I won't be pessimistic, it's just that I think that programmatically, American architecture simply has not been speculating in those terms. I think it is also very much an issue of where the attention of the architecture is going.

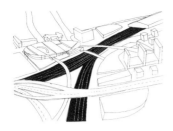

You talked about the similarities between European and American cities. Are there any remaining differences? One of the things I found fascinating about the new towns around Paris is that they are still called new towns, even though some of them are 40 years old. In America that would simply be a town. In terms of their infrastructure, they still have an incredible dependence upon the main body. They all maintain these parasitic relationships, none of them are autonomous. They are conceived as dormitory towns, second-best towns, or towns for immigrants. Nobody who has absolute choice would choose to live there, however. That gives them a melancholy quality.

Right now, these cities could achieve a kind of critical mass and thus acquire their own credibility. Very important for Marne-la-Vallée is the fact that EuroDisney will open there in 1993, demonstrating again that this kind of freedom could never exist in the central city or the classical city. Maybe Disneyland is only an exaggerated metaphor for the potential of those towns—the entertainment, the freedom, the kind of life. A kind of consciousness is developing in the local politicians that, instead of always imagining radial connections, they could completely turn things around with bridge connections among those towns. A metro could connect the centers of the new towns. In isolation, all those places are relatively underprivileged, but strung together, they could form an enormous battery of modern events, modern phenomena, modern conditions, that could be very attractive.

Do you see any changes in the way architecture will be practiced in Europe with the upcoming changes in the EC? I think I am a good example of how it will change the world of architecture. We opened an office in the Netherlands in 1981, but now only 5 percent of our work is in Holland, while 30 percent is in France, 30 percent is in Germany, and 30 percent in Japan. Because we speak German and French and English, we are a typical European practice and maybe a model of the European practice of the future. I have a fixed day in Paris, a fixed day in Germany, and a fixed day in a city in northern France.

Our expansion is exciting because in Holland they don't spend any money on architecture, and architecture plays no role in the self-image of the culture. It used to be very different, but not any more. Holland is nothing but a burned-out skeleton of a culture that was once ambitious, critical, and devoted to a kind of modernism. In those other countries, architecture is seen as a prime manifestation either of the political system or of some other self-image.

Even though there is so much interaction between these countries, they each retain amazing eccentricities and peculiarities, even in architecture. But globalization has changed architecture completely, because we are all thinking in terms of Europe and not in terms of our own countries—almost to the point that everyone is more popular outside his mother country.

One of the characteristics of newer cities is a kind of "monoculture." Is a maturing taking place, making them richer environments?

In Atlanta you can see some maturing going on. You can also see that forms of the public realm, which are in physical terms very different from the classical forms, generate or support intense forms of communication. In that sense it is not necessary that architects worry about the inherent needs or the given characteristics of the human being changing drastically.

*Can architecture give rise to a social consciousness that goes beyond
simply fulfilling the needs of the client?* What is exciting
in Europe right now is that the myth "Europe '92" is in the air. It has
stimulated an enormous amount of speculation, more political than commercial. Because it is political, important new programs are being invented
and new needs are being identified. For once the architect is not in the
humiliating position in which he found himself several years ago, of a lover
who has to advocate his own charms to somebody who is basically not
interested. The situation is now radically different, in the sense that there
are a series of enterprises and for those enterprises only architects
can make amenities—and that is really astonishing. One of the most extrav-
agant examples is the competition that was held for the Bibliothèque de
France. It was a unique moment in the history of architecture for a building
on such a colossal scale to be devoted to communal interests.

In a way we are spoiled now, because our social conscience is not
something we have to worry about applying or not applying, as a kind of
decorative act. We don't have to ask, "Do we put our social conscience on
hold, or do we lobotomize ourselves?" It becomes a crucial part of the
issues we deal with. There is no reason to believe that this is not possible
in America. In Japan, there are enormously ambitious montages of
incredibly complex programs. There is a fantastic layering that ranges from
amusement and entertainment to the most humorless seriousness about

culture that you can possibly imagine. In Japan it is not politics that takes the lead but commercial interests, which are venturing into larger and more complex projects. The same will happen here before long.

I think of optimism as a fundamental position, in the sense that it is almost an implicit obligation of an architect. I cannot imagine an architect who conceives out of anything but optimism, but maybe that is a very naive idea. Since every architect operates on the world, I think it would be obscene if the motivation did not in some way claim its operation would have a beneficial effect, that it would be something good and therefore, ultimately, optimistic.

I am not a really optimistic person. For instance, the project at Melun-Sénart is not necessarily optimistic. It nevertheless tries to reach certain conditions and certain realities in a way that almost artificially imposes a sort of optimism. It is an optimism that supposes the acceptance of conditions. For instance, suppose that 90 percent of our ambitions turn into mud, are flawed, or don't work anymore, or imagine the whole architectural profession is run through a shredder and only tiny fragments of plankton are what remain, the question is can you work with that plankton? Does it offer a basis for something else? My position is a kind of research that perhaps is not so much optimism, but which simply does not allow itself to make an entirely negative reading.

How do you feel about your housing
at Checkpoint Charlie now that the Berlin
Wall is gone?

I feel modest about it.
The first competition was
held in 1983, when the rediscovery of the European city was in the air. The
model for the International Building Exhibition (IBA) was the rediscovery
of the perimeter block, which became dogma. At that time I made a propo-
sition that ran counter the dogma. I argued that it was bizarre to erase,
in the name of History, an important part of the history of Berlin. The history of Berlin is of course the 19th century, but it is also the Second World
War, the reconstruction, and the Wall. It seemed completely superficial
to randomly take one model, say it was perfect, and rebuild the city on those
terms, ignoring World War II, the Cold War, and everything else.

My project was totally different. It was like a modern Pompeii—just
low-rise patio housing that was simply put wherever there was an
empty site, and that could be erased or scrapped if things changed. I had

the notion that in the context of the Wall, which was at that time an extremely sinister and fragile presence, it was insipid to make normal housing. There were architects who had nice diagrams with mezzanines and the sun's rays. I found this appallingly superficial. We were forced to conform in some sense, and so it was a great pleasure to make a building that included Checkpoint Charlie. In the basement was a small museum that talked about the role of the American Army in the maintenance of Berlin. The housing was stacked on top. Our building was superseded by events, and in itself that was very exciting and sobering.

We are now negotiating what should happen on the ground floor. We would like to turn it into a museum of what the Wall was, what the Cold War was, what Checkpoint Charlie was. Unfortunately, that is completely taboo in the new Berlin. Nobody wants to know anything about it. Another alternative is to make it a dance hall.

***What influence does the history of architecture
have on your work?*** It's probably
totally subconscious, but from the first moment I was interested in
architecture, I was also interested in the phenomena of modernity and
modernization. At the same time I was interested in the Russian
Constructivist Ivan Leonidov, in Mies van der Rohe, and in American architecture of the 1920s and 1930s. That interest enabled us to support
our own work and to give it a critical dimension. Over the last ten years,
however, I became suspicious of the fact that Modernism was so
easily accepted in Europe. I also became suspicious of my own motives,
and the more dependent I became on Modernism, the more I came to
dislike what we were doing. Somebody, I believe he was English, recently
said that Modernism was perhaps Europe's Post-Modernism. Once that
formula was launched, it became very painful to us. There were some
personnel changes in the office, and since '86 or '87 our work has become
much more independent. Now, we seek to be openly experimental, we
openly state that we want to invent something new. These may be a dangerous or embarrassing ambition, but I think that in some of our work
we are now taking those risks. Clearly the time is ripe. I'm not saying it can
be done now, but there is an amazing coincidence with all of the
programs that are in the air.

What prospects do you see for the historic cores of older cities?

I think their fate is going to be really dark. A city like Amsterdam is now literally being destroyed by its maintenance in that state. It is a vast tourist trap that in the high season is intolerable for one reason and in the low season is intolerable for other reasons. In that sense, unpopular and ugly cities have a greater future. In Holland, a city like Rotterdam is ten times more interesting or promising. I really like being in an American city where the idea of gentrification is so far on the horizon that it really seems to be immune to it. Maybe this is true here in Houston, where that gives a certain pleasure.

***Do you see the
failure of architecture as an outcome of the system of
architectural education?*** All schools
are surprisingly similar,
and every one is more or less as good as any other. The more schools I see,
the more cynical, or perhaps more reassured, I become of this. There is
one difference, in that the tone in American schools is always more idealistic and much more positive and high-minded than in European schools.
In European schools there is an innate cynicism about almost everything,
which on one hand is healthy, but on the other is silly.

One of the difficulties of being an American is that the substance of
Europe can be interpreted to serve almost any theory with impunity,
with immediate and practical verification. Europe is still a kind of myth, and
the authority of European architecture as an idyllic Eden before the fall
is still deeply ingrained in the minds of American teachers and students.
Of course, we all need models and ideals, but this idealized vision of
Europe is not as strong in Europe, because in Europe everybody knows the
lack of culture, the lack of history, as an everyday effect.

The power of architecture is overestimated. Schools are almost
steered by a collective unconscious, or subconscious; in certain periods
certain issues come to the fore and others are ignored, and a little
later the things that were ignored come to the fore, and then other issues
are forgotten, and so on in a continuous movement. It is only when
individuals put their mark on specific schools and institute a kind of dicta-
torship that you can really see distinct schools of thought. In a way
you are an inevitable part of a general culture, with all the sophistication
and blindness that this implies.

Academies have contributed to dismantle architecture's ambitions,
rather than to exercise them. The whole of Post-Modernism is an incredibly
defeatist movement in that sense. There is a fear of making grandiose
statements, and a fundamental fear of coming back to what every architect
in his most infantile moments believes: that he changes the world. And I
think that this, under the enormous weight of economic respectability, has
been denied by both architects and academies.

You have recently sat on a jury for* Progressive Architecture *magazine.* What do you see in American architecture? It was only
possible for the jury to deal with beautiful little buildings, or very well
done architectures. We are marooned in a hopelessly nostalgic system of
judgment that can only lead to negative conclusions. This hopelessly
backward basis for criticism can never tolerate the kind of energy needed
to reinvent the profession.

An enormous territory of incredibly tasteless, extremely bad, horrify-
ingly complex, or absolutely insane architecture was completely and
systematically ignored. I think there was a fascinating contingent of maybe
50 buildings—buildings done in Japan by Americans, or enormous
complexes in Los Angeles by Michael Graves, or buildings by German
architects in America. They were completely synthetic in their genesis. They
were not buildings by a local architect for a specific culture, at a given

time, but were completely speculative projections by an outsider for a noble site in a distant land, at an incredible scale. You get the impression that this is becoming a very important form of architecture.

I am not the only one doing this kind of stuff all over Europe and in Japan. Globalization will pull all of us completely out of the ground and make us, in a very systematic sense, rootless. It will make us strangers everywhere.

The implications of this sort of future for our profession and the sense of what the new abilities of an architect will have to be were completely repressed and ignored. The only judgments that could be made were judgments of taste and of aesthetics. With that went all of our melancholic notions of loss of public space, loss of urbanity, loss of communication, and so forth.

***Are there poetic notions attached to the void you speak of—
something that you see in the culture?*** It certainly has an
artistic impulse. At the same time it is a mixture of opportunism and poetry, in the sense that the real significance for me is that so many of our
efforts are misdirected and that we try, with incredible energy, to recuper-
ate or resuscitate areas of architecture that are no longer legitimate or
valid. That is why simply surrendering a whole area and at the same time
recovering another one has virtue, simplicity, easiness, optimism almost.
In this sense, it is much easier to leave an area void than to use and build
in an area. It is also outside the consumerist onslaught, bombardment
and encroachment of meaning, signification, and messages. The void claims
a kind of erasure from all the oppression, in which architecture plays an
important part.

Blankness is an important quality that is completely ignored, especially
by architects. It creates a kind of horror at its emptiness, but it is a very
important thing to allow and to come to terms with. Our profession is
indoctrinated to never allow something to remain empty, or undecided, or
undetermined. That goes from the large scale to the small scale. Now
there is an enormous rebirth of detailing. On one hand that is fantastic, but
on the other it creates an incredible feeling of pressure: every chair has a
hundred thousand ideas, an ambition to express something, perhaps the way
it is put together, that simply draws attention to itself. Great attention is
given to the packaging of space, but no attention to the space itself.

64

REM KOOLHAAS: SEMINAR

How does a culture of congestion relate to a culture of consumption? They are at least parallel phenomena. Marshall Berman's book *All That Is Solid Melts Into Air* describes modernization and modernism as a kind of maelstrom, which implies that you have no choice in terms of your fundamental alignment that the surfer has to make with the wave. There is absolutely no obstacle or no inherent possibility of making critical steps or commentary or using it as a critique of certain things. For instance, the library can be seen as a consumer's benefit, but on the other hand it was an idealistic statement, not only by me, but by the French. They ask how there still could be a gesture or an articulation of the public realm, in the face of today's incredible consumerism and an electronic onslaught that tends to dissolve anything physical. In architectural terms, architects are right now looking for a pretext as to why certain things cannot happen and are extremely blocked in terms of discovering potential in existing conditions.

Modernism was always geared toward utopia. Can you reconstitute modernism without utopia? My work is deliberately not utopian: it is consciously trying to operate within the prevalent conditions without the suffering, disagreeing, or whatever other kind of narcissism we have, all of which may be merely a complex series of alibis to justify certain interior failings. So it is certainly critical of that kind of utopian modernism. But it still remains aligned with the force of modernization and the inevitable transformations that are engendered by this project which has been operating for 300 years. In other words, for me the important thing is to align and find an articulation for those forces, again without the kind of purity of a utopian project. In that sense my work is positive vis-à-vis modernization but critical vis-à-vis modernism as an artistic movement.

Flying the Bullet,

or

When Did the Future Begin?

SANFORD KWINTER

A. Toward an Extreme Architecture

To convert optimism into danger and to make that danger speak; this set of operations arguably has always been the core of Rem Koolhaas's architectural program, even as far back as the "Voluntary Prisoners of Architecture" project of 1972. Yet never has it been expressed quite so explicitly as here, in this deceptively small, manifesto-like book, which opens with just such a blunt proclamation: "Architecture is a *dangerous* profession." And although this phrase emerges modestly and deliberately at the outset, with little pretence to impress, the words do not fail, by book's end, to bring home both the dramatic affirmations and the wild defiances implicit in their message. The Koolhaas optimism, then, is twofold: it states not only that architecture must turn away from the comfortable vanity and narcissism that continue to protect it from the hazardous realities of historical becoming, but also that architectural speculation must pragmatically refocus on "discovering [new] potential in existing conditions," on "aligning, and finding articulation for, the inevitable transformations and forces of modernization" (p.65). For Koolhaas, the posture of optimism forms no less than an "obligation," indeed a "fundamental position," for any architecture (p.53); Serious architecture must actually *desire* to be dangerous. Yet the critical question nevertheless remains: How actually to become dangerous? Seen through OMA's work, at least one answer would read in the following manner: Architecture becomes dangerous when it forgoes all that is "pregiven"—in this case fixed types and predetermined matter—when, rather, it takes the actual flow of historical conditions as its privileged materiality (not the habitual discrete domains of geometry, ma-sonry, stone, and glass), and works these, adapts these through transformations and deformations, in order to engender and bind its form. The effect of danger derives here from the fact that this radical view of materiality is a perfectly active, fluid and mobile one: it describes a mate-riality that actually moves and changes as it is worked, one that envelops and releases its own spontaneous properties or traits, carries its own capacities to express itself in form—all beyond the arbitrary reach of external control. This is why for Koolhaas truly radical optimism is incompatible with utopianism: Optimism recognizes an inherent propensity or directedness in *any* disposition of historical things (even the post-historical "fragments" or the passive drift of cultural "plankton" to which Koolhaas alludes), a direction or propensity that may be drawn out and *followed*, while utopianism remains imprisoned within the moral universe of what "ought" to be, and so can call on no materiality whatever on which to impress its chimerical shape. Optimism and danger, very simply, are affirmations of the wildness of *life*—of the life that resides even in places and things—while utopianism remains an affirma-tion of the stillborn universe of the metaphysician's *Idea*: transcendent, fixed, and quixotically indifferent to the vivid roilings of a historical world.

To follow the movements of matter, to seize the prodigious blooms of "work" that emerge "for free" at certain critical moments in matter's free and irregular flow, is to collaborate with, and actually develop, the unfoldings of a vitalist universe, to tap both its powerful inevitability and its vast, though subtle, *potential*; to merge with that fluid universe, to both guide and be guided by its unchallengeable, inexhaustible, but fully intuitable efficacy. All technology depends at one level or another on the harnessing of just these types of potential forces, although for the most part we have forgotten that that is where its power and poetry lie. Thus modern techno-science happily operates on an arid continuum of numbers (or on skillfully reduced matter-models designed to behave like a pristine, controlled numerical milieu), willfully oblivious that the flow of numbers through equations only approximately reproduces, yet certainly entirely derives from, the more primitive and far more inventive flows of real matter. Though these processes today remain largely hidden from us, the pre-modern "arts" of intuition—ancient (and most current) metallurgy, nautical and telluric wayfinding, agriculture, plant pharmacology, astronomy, medical semeiotics, etc.—all depended on the ability to apprehend multiple dynamic trajectories in space-time as distinct stratifications in a single organic ensemble. The trick, then as now, is to grasp both together—both the whole and the nested passages that we moderns analytically refer to as "parts"—to know that materiality is but a continuous production of properties vigorously yet compliantly seeking to integrate into new complexes, alloys, and alliances. By manipulating the focus, viscosity, direction, and "fibrosity" of these material flows, complex natural or artificial reactions take place, and from this, the "new" and the unexpected suddenly become possible. All *techné* is at bottom the husbanding and manipulation of these fluid relations to produce new shapes of order.

Although this fluid art of variation and husbandry is by no means "lost," it is clearly no longer the province of modern thinking.[1] As the world continues to vary and flow, to aggregate, self-organize, and to re-break apart, most modern humans operate within a gridded metaworld of abstraction, ratiocination, and the crudest approximations to nature that even the most massive number-crunching devices cannot exceed. As a result most modern architecture draws its form, not from the topological world of fluid materiality, but from the rigid metaworld of ideality, of hubristic (naive) machinism, and of dead geometry. This arrested world, blind to the dimensions of time, produces an equally blind architecture, an architecture thrown from the metaworld into the real one, like a lead boot into time's refreshing river. There are simply no corresponding hooks or currents to keep it afloat.

While almost anything workaday—though also mediocre—is possible from within such a schema, everything exceptional, all true innovation, necessarily draws from the other side. Whatever depends on rote repeatability or on a uniformity of relations in space and time to achieve its effect will find its cause well supported by the time- and material-blind world of abstract operations. The "new"—by definition that which deviates or departs from what has already appeared—is, however, the offspring of creative, material instabilities cultivated beyond the looking-glass of the grid; it seems that we cannot help but explain novelty to ourselves (although this almost certainly betrays a false consciousness) as a dispatch from a mythical "outside." But this "outside" is in fact everywhere, all around us, indeed ours for the conjuring up. In the modern world we witness it most acutely in "extreme" conditions of performance, in real-time engagement with a wildly mobile environment in frenetic material flux. All extreme sports, for example—skysurfing, bungee ballet, base jumping, BMX, speedclimbing, etc.—have for an ethos the concept of *a limit that must be reached and inhabited*, a performative destination known as "the ragged edge."[2] It is not by accident that such images abound: the liminal condition is in fact a communicative interface where rational information processing (i.e. planning) breaks down under the weight of too many, and too quickly shifting, variables, where it then gives way to spontaneous *material* intelligences ("intuition" in philosophy, "universal computation" in science), to the archaic way of proceeding by feel and by flow and by following the grain of the world-unfolding—to the process of *becoming material* oneself. It is said that at the edge we encounter danger, but this is just another way of saying that there we are forced to communicate critically with a great many dimensions at once.

Nowhere is the necessity of opening oneself up, and remaining attuned, to a multiplicity of dimensions more critical than in the world of aerial combat. Since the enumeration of German ace Oswald Boelcke's eight "dicta" of 1916, the principles of aerial warfare have undergone refinement, but they have not changed. Tactical rules for mobile weaponry were, of course, already both commonplace and remarkably sophisticated as developed over centuries of marine warfare by French, Spanish, and especially British admirals. But naval maneuvers, for all their elegance and complexity, lack two a priori dimensional constraints that strongly condition aerial ones. Although in the maritime milieu one must account not only for the positions of enemy ships, their relation to land and nearby fleets, supply times, and routes, but for wind and water currents as well, the entire choreography plays itself out on a single surface, in only two dimensions of space. Also, the use of strategic immobility remains a clear, and still effective, option in sea control, and has been so from the time of the famous Beachy Head battle between the Earl of Torrington and the Comte de Tourville in 1690, when the former, although he lost the battle for Britain (and most of the Dutch fleet

under his command), invented the doctrine of the "fleet in being," according to which one deploys one's forces geometrically in such a way
as to paralyze action yet project a continuous threat. Combat in the air,
of course, takes place fully in three spatial dimensions, and immobility does not figure as an option—one chooses simply to engage the
enemy, or not. But these are still only rudimentary givens. Aerial
warfare has its own specific features, of which speed, or total fluidity, is
the primary one.

For Koolhaas, the concept of "America" has always loomed large.
It not only has served enormous aesthetic ends but has played a major
role in generating both the novelty and the radicality in OMA's work
(especially in the primarily European context with which it has dealt), and
has provided a coherent theoretical framework through which the OMA
office has come to understand and harness, for speculative architectural
and urbanistic ends, the volatile processes of late-capitalist modernization. For Koolhaas, America, although deeply studied and assimilated into
his work, has always strategically been kept at a "dangerous"—and
therefore creative—distance: it has been constituted and skillfully main-
tained as the necessarily ragged, mythical gateway to the destabilizing,
novelty-inducing outside. Koolhaas's America (Houston, Atlanta,
Manhattan) would come to represent the whoosh of matter in free action,
wellspring of the new, provenance of everything that has ever carried

the wishful promise of "the future"—a strange and extreme milieu—
a domain of pure movement free of historical drag. It was this America
that actually invented the hyper-future, precisely because only
America could invent the outside of the outside. Europe invented "Amerika"
as *their* future and outside, but America invented the new frontiers—
outer space and the insane warp speed that was meant to take them
there—as theirs. Speed and space were the new materials of which
the future would be made.

Among architects, then, Koolhaas is the true American, for he is the
only one to have attempted to engage the absolute and pure future.
And yet, from where does this strange idea of a pure future come? After
the Second World War, America rode a manic wave of cocksureness,
not so much for having won a war as for having realized the hubristic
technological achievement that made such a claim possible in the
first place: the Manhattan Project and its colossal, savage product, the
Atom Bomb. The American air force played a crucial role in choreograph-
ing this complex, two-year long gesture, which was said to be
capable of ending all wars; its pilots had also performed brilliantly in many
critical battles in both the European and Asian theaters. Returning
home after the war, the flying aces were celebrated as godlike heroes, and
the warmasters soon decided that the sci-fi, bigger-than-real postwar
future would be ushered in on their shoulders (and at the risk of their

necks). To maintain America's technological (geopolitical) edge, it was decided that two fundamental space-time "barriers" would have to be torn down: a manned aircraft would need to fly beyond the outer limit of the earth's atmosphere (280,000 feet), and the so-called sonic wall— Mach 1 (660 to 760 miles per hour)—the speed beyond which, it was commonly believed, any aircraft would disintegrate—had somehow to be surpassed. These linked achievements laid the foundations for what the general public would soon—deliriously—come to know as the space race.

There was one pilot whose wartime dogfighting skills and natural aircraft handling abilities were legendary, indeed considered by some to be supernatural. For these reasons Chuck Yeager was chosen after the war to spearhead the classified supersonic project, and by October 1947 he had broken the proverbial sound barrier, against the advice and conventional wisdom of many physicists. But Yeager could know what no physicist ever could: he was a pure creature of movement and speed, among the most instinctive pilots the air force has ever seen. "The only pilot I've ever flown with who gives the impression that he's part of the cockpit hardware, so in tune with the machine that instead of being flesh and blood, he could be an autopilot. He could make an airplane talk."[3] In the space-time world of the dogfight, where Yeager's instincts were trained, everything takes place right at the limit, perhaps even a little beyond. To survive "you've got to fly an airplane close to the ragged edge where you've got to keep it if you really want to make that machine talk." Knowing the critical tolerances of the aircraft in a variety of violent, dangerous maneuvers was everything. One had to know exactly "where the outside of the envelope was . . . [to] know about the part where you reached the outside and then *stretched* her a little . . . without breaking through."[4] Aerial dogfighting, more than anything else, is like space-time arbitrage: one must exploit discrepancies that appear between parallel flows (the twisting vectors of adversarial aircraft). But these flows are so far from equilibrium—so stretched—that the critical discrepancies must be snatched from any dimension that is not already totally strained to the max. No one knew this "fine feathered edge" better than Yeager.[5]

There are many ways to inhabit space, and so there are many ways to handle an airplane. In Koolhaas, I will want to claim, we bear witness not only to a remarkable architectural project traditionally defined but to the emergence of a new way of holding social and economic space altogether, for which, in architecture, there are no real precedents at all.[6] Koolhaas's work, with its fierce, stark geometries and imperious logic, is in many senses an *extreme architecture*, and bears philosophical and ontological kinship with all extremity (even virtual or unrealized) in all domains of cultural activity. What these extreme states and activities have in common is sudden precipitation and total blending of diverse materialities, of wild fluxes, in an organic computational ensemble that defies both predetermination and "hard," or rational, control ("If you have to think, you're dead," according to a common fighter pilot's slogan). In simpler terms, extreme activities involve the mobilization of every inter-acting part in a field, so that every movement of every part instan-taneously changes the conditions of the unfolding of the whole. The edge of the envelope is where time (relations) gains the computational upper hand over space (things).

In Yeager's world, the sky is a totally kinetic domain. One could say that Koolhaas's work is to classical architecture exactly what the dogfight is to formation flying. In the air, formations establish rigid, homo-geneous structures of movement and relationship. They inject a uniformity into space by fixing intervals and relative speeds, and arrest natural variation and all developmental routines. Even the earth, the sun, and the horizon are drawn into this meticulous stratification, for they are all interpreted as stable, on their own and in relation to one another: the earth's varying features serve as guides on which to project fixed routes, the horizon equilibrates gravity like a regulating line, and the sun offers a fixed point to triangulate position and the progress of linear movement. In air-to-air combat this space becomes not only liquid but turbulent: the sun, the earth, and the horizon spin, volley, and fly—in a phrase, they go ballistic. The pilot episodically *uses* these elements (and their ballistic pathways) to hide against, to blind the opponent, or to create vertiginous relationships of weaving, gyrating motion. The cardinal rule for survival in aerial combat: *Never become predictable.* What better slogan for the creation of a truly modern—and wild—architecture? Imagine a fighter (History/Capital) on your tail. You are forced into evasive maneuvers to avoid getting "locked" on the radar intercept screen. Do you now follow guidebook escape routes? Regularly shaped oscillating trajectories? Do you carve desultory, fluctuating lines across a single, even skewed plane? Certainly not. The true problem is how to avoid *any* regular repetitive behavioral pattern (how to depart the space you are in entirely)? The simple but not obvious solution is: *Explode into all dimensions at once.* Easier to say than to do? Perhaps, but far from impossible. All three of the projects Koolhaas has presented here—the multiple, focused confluences of communication, transport, and capital flows of the Zeebrugge vortex; the plucked and twisted, then re-embedded, positive-negative and scoop-the-loop structures of the Bibliothèque de France; the psycho-plastic amplifications of image and infrastructure in the Karlsruhe Art and Media Center—represent exactly such controlled explosions of active materiality into invisible but adjacent co-dimensions. [End encounter number one: History/Capital disengages, peeling off into a long arc, circling back to re-engage later in a different tactical scenario.]

In November 1994, Yeager published a brief article on air-combat tactics. The article consisted of three short paragraphs, each outlining what might be referred to as three new "dicta" on how to expand the elastic "edge" of any "envelope."[7] Before examining these dicta, it is worth pointing out how the envelope concept is itself significant. The term's origin almost certainly derives from military ergonomic milieus, a context in which "envelope" always implies at least three things: the idea that a human-machine interface constitutes a next-order synthetic unity; the idea of a homeostatically contained group of forces in flux that form a temporary, fluid, but *historical* ensemble; and the idea that this unity or ensemble is an organic one, that it is defined *performatively*, and possesses its own global tolerances and parameters. The envelope, by definition, is a communicative, active apparatus. No wonder it has for years been a favorite term in Koolhaas's lexicon. A Koolhaas project, for better or worse, is never an eternal or stable solution to a "classic" problem, nor does it pretend to be. Rather, it is a provisional, elastic resolution of a compound conjunctural *situation*. His solutions have half-lives, they are temporally and historically determined, they move with the stream of the world and so build in flexibility and allow for immense programmatic turnover. They are more fully products of their n-dimensional *epoch* than of their time-blind (world-blind!), literal *site*. The Koolhaas work, like the aerial encounter, is composed in a purely tactical arena, formed in an abstract envelope of concrete historical (cosmopolitan) fluids.

B. The Full Metal Jacket

See more than your opponent sees: Yeager dictum number 1. For the flyer this can mean only one thing: free the eyes of objects and the habits that follow from object-oriented vision. Yeager shows how to retrain one's focus to take in all of space, to see everything. (When asked what made him such an exceptional flyer, Yeager used to answer, "I had the best eyes.") For the architect, this means take your focus to infinity, do not linger on objects but rather enter the space tactilely and prospect the space in search of breaking developments. Scan for changes and fluctuations, then respond as if part of a cycle, as if you had always been a causal part of those flows. This dictum works well with the more classic exhortation to "spot the enemy first." Arbitrage, here as everywhere, is the process that makes the emerging difference critical—the symmetry break that "seeds" space, allowing form to rush in. For Yeager, as for Koolhaas, history, even material history, is all about thresholds. This is because in free matter, energy and information become perfectly coextensive fluxes, the translation of one into the other is simultaneous, and events are "computed" instantly. Matter, like history, is an aggregate, partly fluid and partly solid, a "colloid" or liquid crystal that shifts its pattern rhythmically in relation to the flow of inputs and outputs that traverse it. The shifts are distributed like stages with triggers that are tripped when variables extend beyond their local "equilibria," or envelopes. The pilot must learn to enter this domain as free matter, to become computationally coextensive with the aggregate's unfolding, so that all reaction is instantaneous ("If you have to think, you're dead"). Koolhaas's technique is to ride these thresholds as well. After all, "threshold" is just another name for that privileged event-filled place at the edge of the envelope.[8] In the present book, he defines at least six thresholds or emergences, potential or already realized: *congestion*, short of which the "metropolitan" effect would not exist; *a new concept of Europe*, its new modalities of collecting, storing, and deploying energy based on a sudden "explosion of scale," and the multiple reorganizations that take place around it; *bigness*, the umbrella theme that typifies all "quantum" phenomena in the late-modern landscape, where changes in scale and size produce not only changes in degree but changes in kind (new qualities); *dissociation of interior and exterior*, which become not only autonomous programs and domains to be developed freely, but free-floating values (exteriority folded within buildings; interiorities, as in a Riemannian manifold, locally and promiscuously defined); *sheer mass as affect or trait*, a density-volume relationship, like Jorge Silvetti's "Colossal,"[9] that speaks a forgotten language, like a lost tribe of the Beautiful suddenly come home; and *rootlessness*, the severing of relations with slow and deep unfoldings (the old-world swells of "ground" and "place") and the reterritorialization—inevitable if regrettable—onto the "fast, cheap, and out of control" ethos of late-modern capital, demographics, and globalization.[10]

Yeager's third dictum (allow me to save the second for last): *Use all four dimensions*. A poor pilot (and a mediocre architect) thinks of space as a discrete manifold of two-dimensional sheets in a variety of different axes and orientations. An average pilot (and a better architect) thinks in terms of three dimensions in continuum. In a dogfight, however (or in the space of the late twentieth century), a precise and especially a plastic sense of time is critical. What most pilots don't understand, Yeager tells us, is that "by controlling the throttle, they're controlling *time*."[11] Time, of course, is not simply one dimension among others; it is *the dimension out of which all other dimensions unfold*. It is adjacent to everything, it presses at every edge, assigns every threshold, opens onto every becoming. How long does it take to get from point A to point B? That question is at the basis of modern material space, although not in the sense of a simple translatory trajectory. In a four-dimensional manifold, space, quite simply, is alive. Points A and B are no longer simple coordinates in a Newtonian *lattice* ("simple location," in Whitehead's terminology), but vectors in a Lagrangian *mesh* (Whitehead's proto-"organism"). What this means is that every movement drags local space along with it—local conditions with a high degree of correlation with their surroundings—so that every displacement of location is simultaneously a transformation of kind. In the dogfight—an extreme activity par excellence, because time becomes so material you

can taste it—the variables become so multiplied that the very concept of
aerial tactics essentially evaporates.[12] All that is left is a very rapid game
of "relative motion and time-distance problems." This new, Lagrangian
space is one of compound correlations or, in aerial combat, of "multiple
tactics." For example, with several enemy and friendly aircraft in play,
you must, in a given situation, determine whether you can take an enemy
off your wingman's tail even while another is already coming, and gun-
ning at you. You must compute the "energy" differential in each "frame":
can your relative motion get you into range to take out one aircraft
before the relative motion of the fighter on your tail can get into range to
take you? In such a situation, it must be remembered, speed determines
every coordinate (not "simple location"), yet velocity remains only a
relative value. The game is to exploit differentials, and to produce them
when needed, continually, and indeed literally, out of thin air. For
example, forcing an opponent to overspeed is even more effective than
flying pirouettes around him. This logic explains why the slower Russian
and Chinese MiGs had tighter turning radiuses, why they enveloped a
different spectrum of traits or "materiality," and why this made them lethal
to many much faster aircraft. In encounters such as high-speed turns,
for example, the appearance of significant G forces introduced a new inter-
nal envelope, with new tolerances that offered a new material dimension that could be exploited, a new envelope to be feathered or stretched.

The envelope of fluids that presents itself to the fighter pilot is not simply one of multiple mobile elements—the diverse aptitudes of his own airplane, the positions and energy levels of terrain, horizon, sky, sun, enemy, co-wingmen, etc.—whose coordination must be precisely tracked; it is one of compound relationships all woven together in hyper-time. The architect who grasps this grasps the bizarre truth of both the dogfight and of late capitalism all at once: the agent who triumphs is the one who makes best use of his aircraft and weapons within the constraints of its performance envelope. One must fly one's airplane closer to the edge of the envelope (without exceeding it) than the opponent—History/ Capital—flies its. One materiality against another, in the same world, with freedom hovering alongside disaster, just at the edge. Optimism and danger: two heads on the shoulders of a single beast.

This brings us to the final problem of intergrating gunnery into the flight system, and with it Yeager's final, most mystical, dictum: *Fly the bullet*. Learning to see and learning to shoot, it turns out, are extremely similar problems, the latter at an order of magnitude and complexity a full step above the former. Yet as we move up the ladder of complexity, we also move up the ladder of integration: more elements in interaction but with a smoother overall shape. Lars Lerup has written of "megashapes," algorithmic ghosts buried in geometrical systems that offer themselves to the intuition, albeit parceled over time.[13] Others have spoken of strange emergences, where "prehensions" occur replete with control mechanisms that remain demonstrably stable but cannot be located in the system's parts. This is the case even with simple swarm and flock activity in animal continuums. Again, the smoothness of the flow-shape is what strikes both the mind and the eye. This smoothness actually derives from the intense *directedness* that is built into material systems. One could again invoke the theoretical intricacies of the Lagrangian mesh, but for such a complex problem duty obliges one to develop a much simpler model. We are again dealing with relative motion and time/distance computation: how to make the bullet find the enemy aircraft, or rather, how to make the bullet meet its target, in time and not only in space . . . when that rendezvous must clearly take place in the unknowable future! This was the same problem, at another level, on which Norbert Wiener worked during World War II and which led to the science of cybernetics. But long before the science of cybernetics there was the art of cybernetics. Now the art remains superior to the science in most extreme (hypertemporal) situations and milieus, and so it is the art that both the pilot and the visionary architect pursue. How, then, to fly the bullet? Well, Yeager was probably a natural:

> In the midst of a wild sky, I knew that dogfighting was what I was born to do.
> It's almost impossible to explain the feeling: it's as if you were one with that

mustang, an extension of that damned throttle. . . . You were so wired into that airplane that you flew it to the limit of its specs. . . . You felt that engine in your bones, felt it nibbling toward a stall, getting maximum maneuvering performance . . . achieved mostly by instinctive flying: you knew your horse. [14]

No, this is not mysticism; it is computational metallurgy. We all know that metals are liquids whose flow has been arrested. Precisely where and by what sequence of operations we arrest them determines how these metals will behave, what they look like, and what qualities they possess. The closer we bring them to extreme states—that is, liquid, compressed, or hot—the more qualities or properties they "speak." Arresting their various flows is a process achieved through painstaking operations, separating this one off, letting these others continue on for one or two more measures. Artisans in all materials follow and exploit the found material pattern and structure that presents itself as "potential"—the work for free spoken of above. Even fish tap the vortexes in their aquatic environment in a similar way to achieve greater than 100 percent locomotor efficiency. Mostly, though, this work emerges at confluences, where communication and information exchange between systems is at its most intense.

Yeager has taught generations of pilots how to fly and be effective in the air. There is no doubt that these techniques, these modes of extracting effects from unfolding configurations, are transmissible. Fly the bullet: "In order to lead the [enemy] plane [on its time path so your bullets will meet it], you have to be able to make the aircraft an extension of your body."[15] Now the submerged art of cybernetics has always said, Your airplane is metal. Your flight path is metal. (Our cities, no doubt, are metal!) Of course the airplane is very complex metal, exceptionally highly organized and, of course, full of life. Now that it is "hot" enough—that is, far enough from equilibrium and therefore close to the envelope's edge—hadn't we really ought to let its own metallic nature speak? The entire encounter now, including your nervous system, is a metallic one (action-potential cycles of Na^+, K^+ and Cl^-), and we must let its metal speak as well. All that remains is to *enter* the imbroglio and *follow* the flow. But to do this we must first forget the airplane.[16] As your focus opens, the airplane is drawn inside you (the universe is metal!).[17] Yeager:

> Don't even think about turning. Just turn your head or your body and let the plane come along for the ride. When you take aim, *fly the bullet into position*.[18]

That's it. Ignore the plane, just fly *the bullet* into position. The sweep of your head and the arc along which your buttocks swing on the cockpit seat form a single computational matrix with the tangent from your guns. Total continuity, total extension into time. There is no room here

for number crunching, no room for computers, no room for auto-override.
"Forget planning," Koolhaas tells us, "Forget the plane," says Yeager.
And we know they are right, because the essence of successful dogfighting, despite radical technological developments, has not changed since
World War I.[19] When Koolhaas cautiously promotes "a forward-looking
extrapolation" (p.47) as an alternative to fixing rules, you know he is
looking for just this extension into the future and into time. Koolhaas's
city is the metallic city (Karlsruhe—the tungsten and phosphorus of the
cathode ray tube; Paris—silver bromide and Technicolor chemistry of
optical image processing; Zeebrugge—the sheet metal of train, boat and
automobile). It is the *cybernetropolis* of "the open" and of the ragged
edge. To fly the bullet is to prime matter with action potential (ionic differentials allowing signals to propagate long distances through the
nervous system by exploiting local interactions), with continuums of influence transmitted ahead of them like shock waves into time.[20] When
Koolhaas talks of the possibility of generating virtual congestion by
eschewing the usual radial connections in favor of circulation and of ser-
ial—or massively parallel—links in a megalopolis condition (what he
calls "bridge connections"), it is just this "action potential" in the urban
axons that he is exploiting. To fly the bullet is to endow the material
field with directedness—all that, and yet nothing mystical, nothing more.

   Koolhaas commits to the bullet and its mysteriously correlated trajectory when he commits to the "vitality," however strange, of what *is*. Vitality *is* materiality, and materiality, like Nietzsche's Will to Power, must always engage other units of itself. Oswald Boelcke makes an important point about Nature as well as dogfighting when in dictum number 6 he says, "If your opponent dives on you, do not try to evade his onslaught, but fly to meet it." Koolhaas, to the horror of many bystanders in the so-called "Resistance," has largely adopted this activist creed.

Vitality, then, is a field property, a quality of active ensembles (of "excitable media" in the biological sense, the "wild sky" in Yeager), and is not reduceable or locatable in the living system, be it that of the city, the organism, or the hyper-field of the dogfight. Life may be defined as a pattern sustaining itself over time, a control system that regulates a sequence of processes that follow mysteriously from one another. In this organismal view of things that, I would claim, we see in both Yeager and Koolhaas, and indeed at every ragged edge through which the future intrudes, there can be no *horror vacuii*. The void, as Koolhaas recognizes, is the very source of novelty, of creative potential, because it is both indeterminate *and* correlated (directed but not predetermined) (p.63). To fly the bullet is to allow the vector, once released, to inhabit itself; it is the interval in the throes of becoming substance. In the organismal view of the world, interval *is* substance, an active plastic medium projected ahead of the present, and which in turn receives it. We do not know in advance what it will be, because it is pure formation (potential) without form.

Only when architecture fully grasps the intuition of continuity and of relation as a pragmatics and as a physics will it have become *extreme*. At that moment, however distant, we may well find that, in architecture, the future did in fact begin with Koolhaas.

Notes

1   On husbandry or the "pastoral" in urban systems generally, and in Koolhaas specifically, see my "Politics and Pastoralism," *Assemblage* 28 (1995).

2   Other extreme sports such as the triple Ironman, ultra-deep-sea diving with liquid inhalants, or unassisted oxygenless ascents to the peak of Everest are also extreme by virtue of their "catastrophic" use of the human body's performance envelope—pushing it to the edge of unconsciousness so that an "autopilot" mechanism must kick in.

3   Major Gen. Fred J. Ascani, in Chuck Yeager, *Yeager*, (New York: Bantam Books, 1985).

4   *Yeager*; Tom Wolfe, *The Right Stuff*, (New York: Bantam Books, 1979).

5   Yeager, who flew only winged aircraft (even the F-104 had seven-foot-long razor wings) or ones that took off under their own power (not including the X-10 experiments of the 1940s), never actually flew beyond the absolute atmospheric boundary (280,000 feet), but he unquestionably prepared the way. He was the first American to probe the extreme edge of the NF-104's envelope (a conventional atmosphere-dependent aircraft) by flying it above 100,000 feet, a test flight that all but cost him his life. Nonetheless, Yeager routinely took his students up beyond the first atmospheric boundary (70,000 feet) where the sky goes black and silent but the air's molecular structure still sustains aerodynamic buoyancy—to give them a taste of the "outside"—that is, of *space*.

6   Sant'Elia, Hilberseimer, and certain early Soviet revolutionaries are among the only figures whose work comes to mind.

7   General Chuck Yeager, "How to Win a Dogfight," *Men's Health*, November 1994. My thanks to Brian Boigon for alerting me to this article.

8   "Class four behaviour" in Stephen Wolfram; "poised systems" and "edge of chaos" in Chris Langton and Stuart Kaufmann; "separatrices" and "catastrophe sets" in Ralph Abraham and René Thom; "bifurcation regimes" and "far from equilibrium states" of chaologists and thermodynamicists; "singularities" in Deleuze and Guattari; "flow" in Csikszentmihalyi and optimal experience theorists; "one-over-f" systems in signal theory; the state of "highest or fulfilled tension" in Zen Buddhist disciplines . . . the list is beautiful, and long.

9   Jorge Silvetti, "The Seven Wonders of the World," a lecture delivered at the Rhode Island School of Design, 1982. A revised version is forthcoming in *Assemblage*.

10 Koolhaas's own *mot d'ordre* here is "fuck context." Cf. "Bigness" in Rem Koolhaas, *S,M,L,XL* (New York: Monacelli Press, 1996).

11 "How to Win a Dogfight." Emphasis supplied.

12 Peter Kilduff with Lieutenants Randall H. Cunningham and William P. Driscoll, "McDonnell F-4 Phantom," in *In the Cockpit*, ed. Anthony Robinson (London: Orbis, 1979). My thanks to Jesse Reiser for bringing this text to my attention.

13 Lars Lerup, "Stim and Dross," *Assemblage* 25 (1994).

14 *Yeager*.

15 "How to Win a Dogfight."

16 Similarly, in the art of juggling, the flexible control of multiple non-linear variables (hands, balls and their trajectories) to maintain a solid pattern is properly achieved only by keeping the eye *off* the ball, that is, by letting touch, memory, and more

importantly, natural rhythmic attractors (coupled oscillator phenomena) deep in the body's bio-schema take over regulating the movements. There is a musical materiality that juggling calls out of the body. The structure of these pattern relationships is just beginning to undergo experimental notation in what is known as "site swap theory." See Peter J. Beek and Arthur Lewbel, "The Science of Juggling," *Scientific American*, November 1995.

17 "Not everything is metal, but metal is everywhere. Metal is the conductor of all matter. . . . *Nonorganic Life* was the invention, the intuition of metallurgy." Gilles Deleuze and Felix Guattari, *A Thousand Plateaus* (Minneapolis: University of Minnesota Press, 1987). The entire discussion of materiality here is indebted to this work, especially the chapters "On Nomadology" and "The Geology of Morals."

18 "How to Win a Dogfight."

19 The RIO (radio intercept officer), who sits directly behind the pilot in most advanced fighters today and who is responsible for managing the weapons systems, has an entirely computerized cockpit. In front, however, computers are often little more than a liability; in aerial combat there never has been such a thing as a push-button war. Even today, bomber pilots seek maximum override capability against automated pilot functions, giving the pilot maximum control over critical "edge" maneuvers. The role of computers, more often than not, is to filter and minimize the flow of numerical data to the pilot's nervous system.

20 Kinematic wave theory, applied to traffic flow studies, has shown that pulses, or traffic shock waves, form on highway traffic clusters. These waves travel backward or forward along the flow entirely independent of, and at a speed greater than, that of any individual automobile or the velocity of the group flow.